THIS POOPING ANIMALS COLORING BOOK

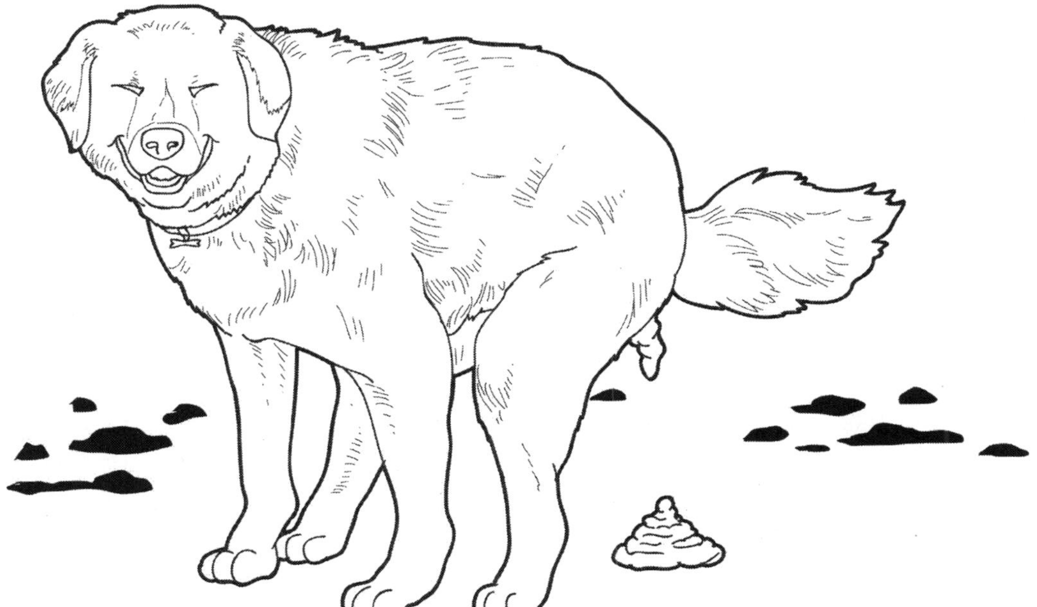

BELONGS TO:

First edition: 2019

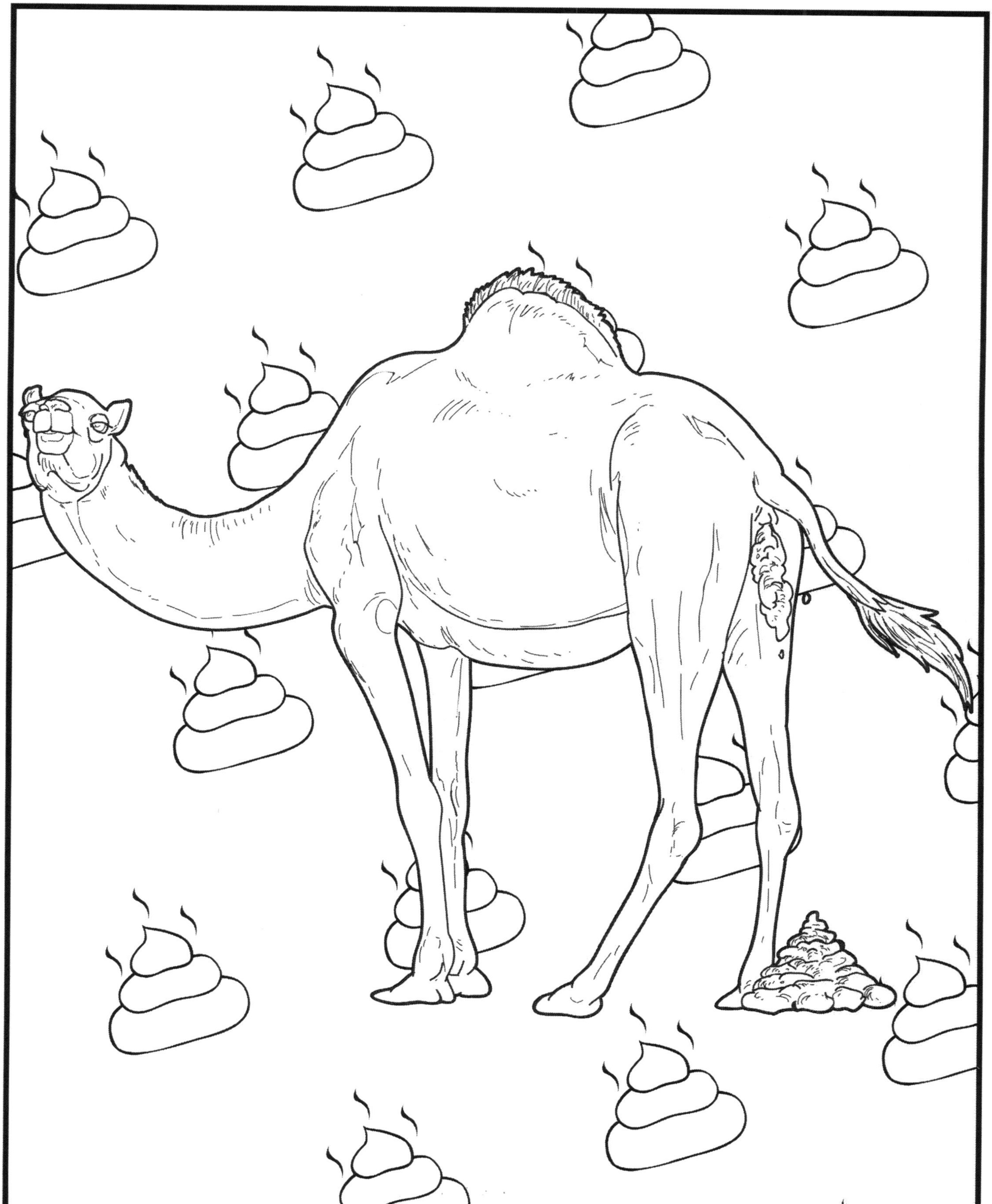

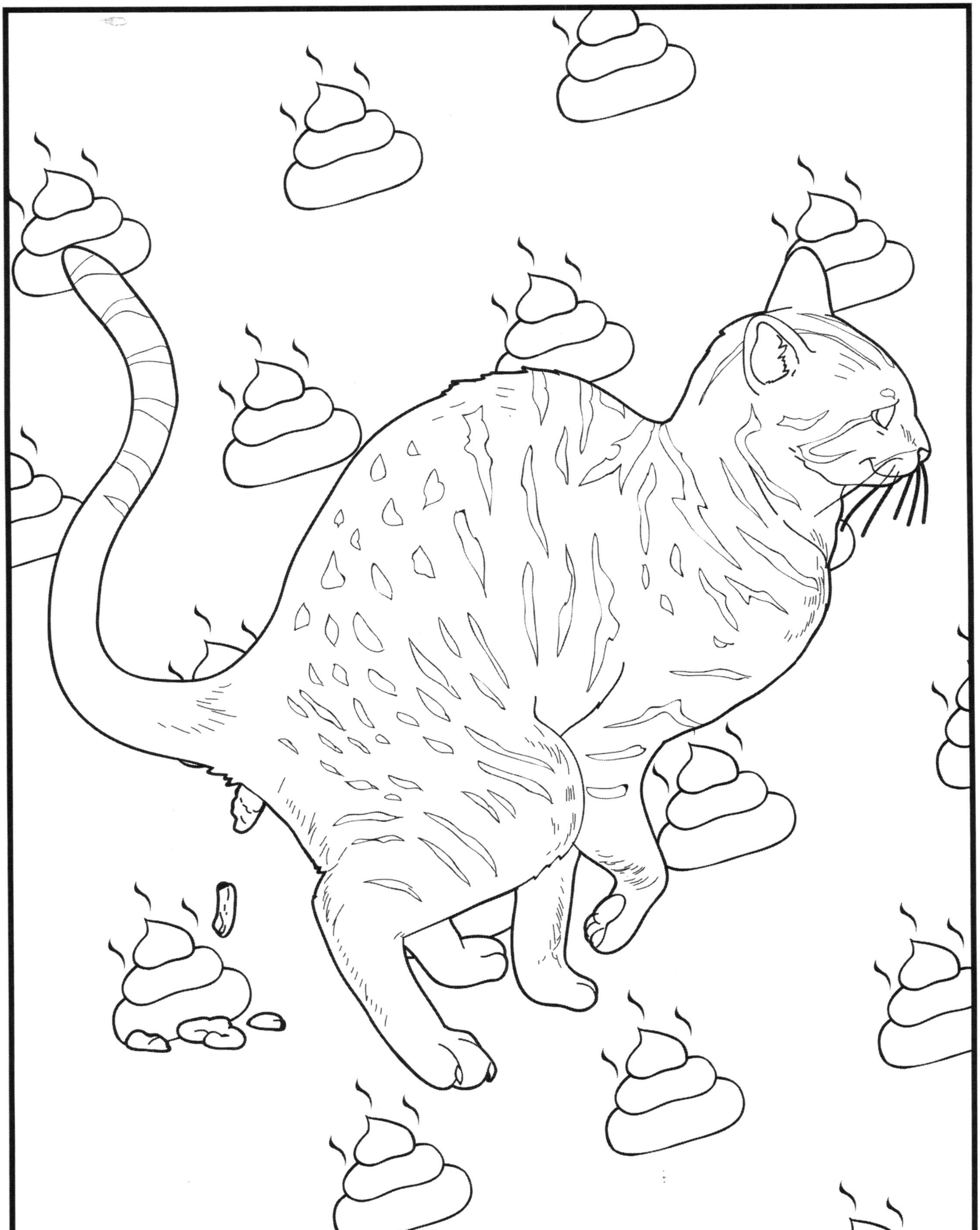

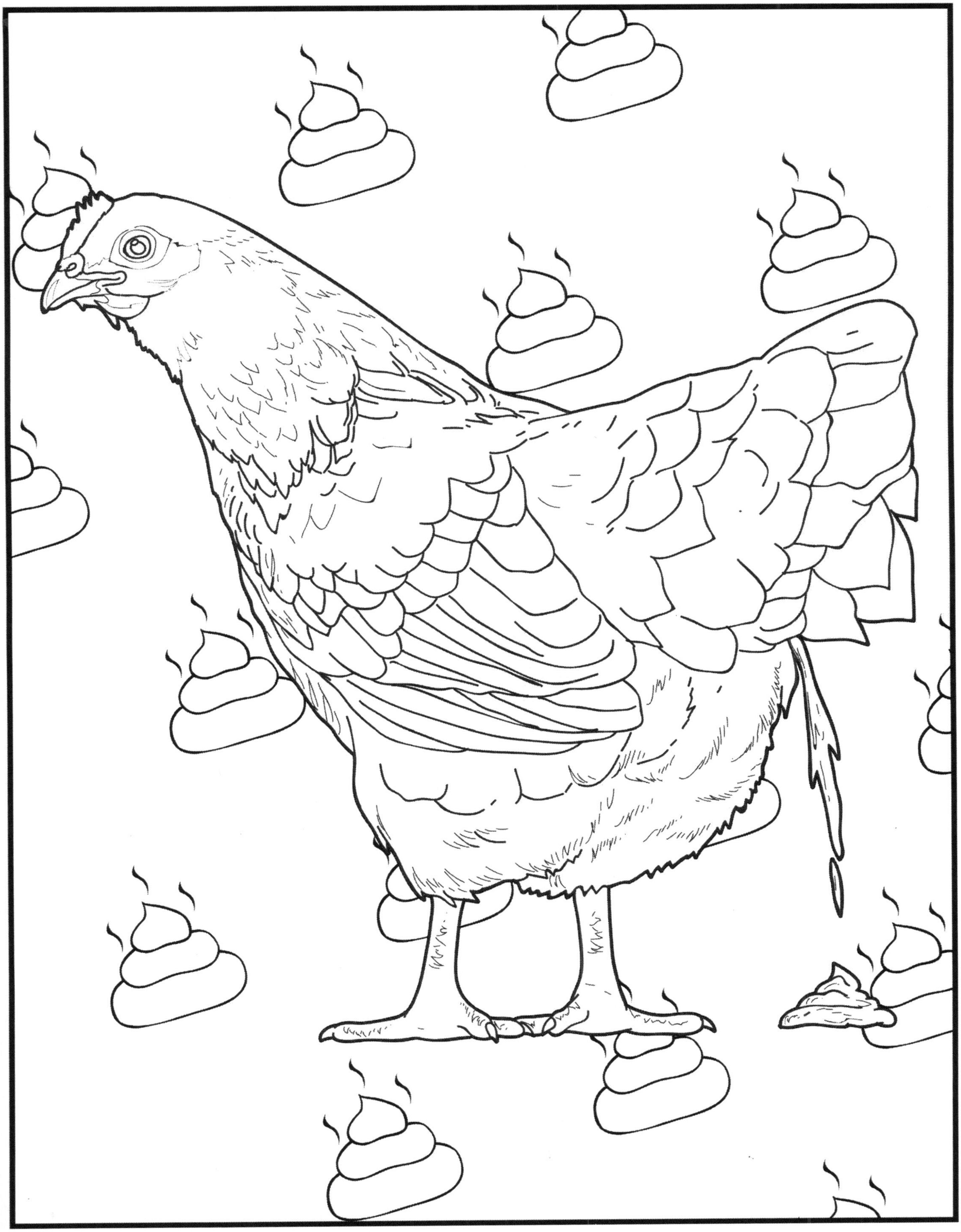

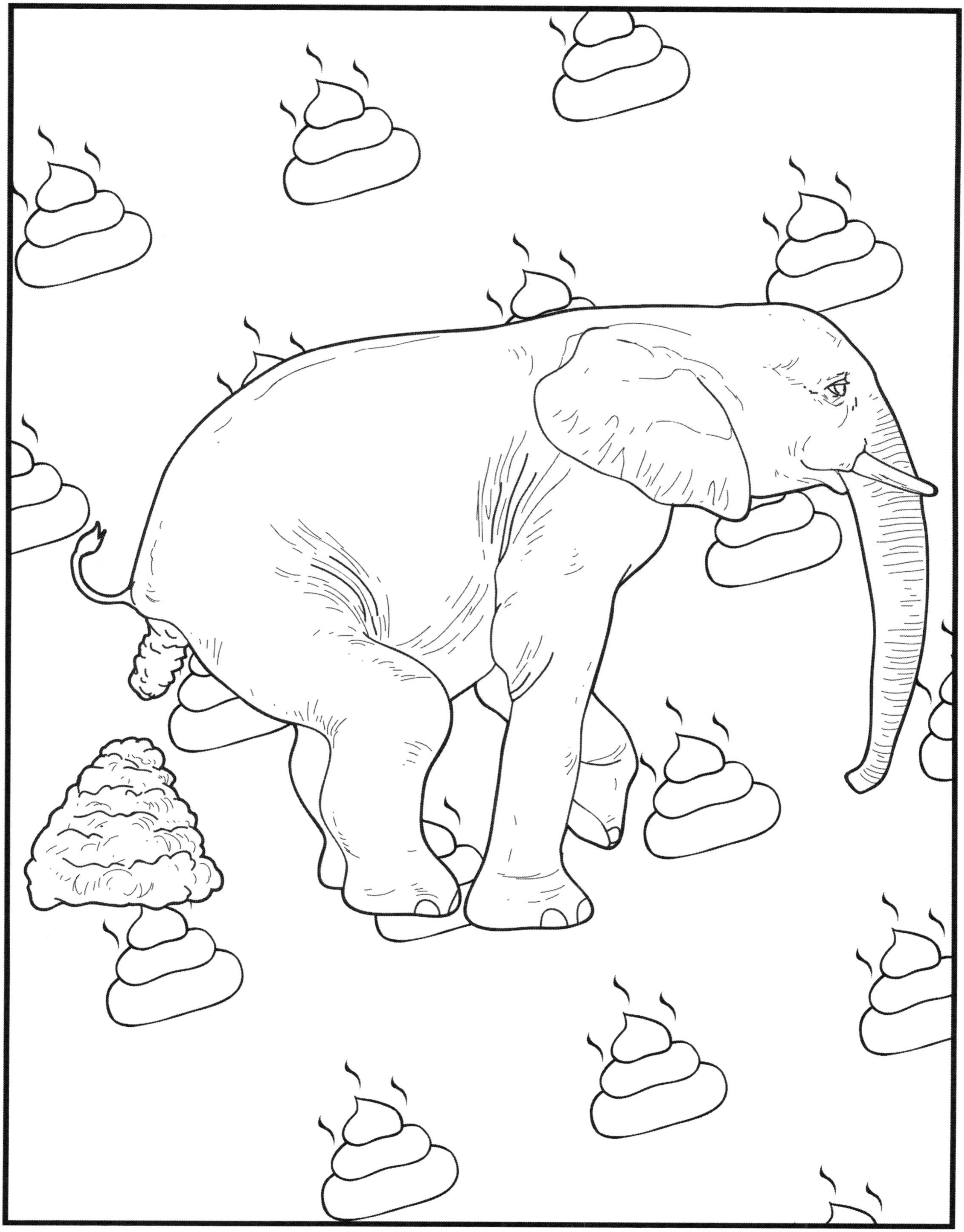

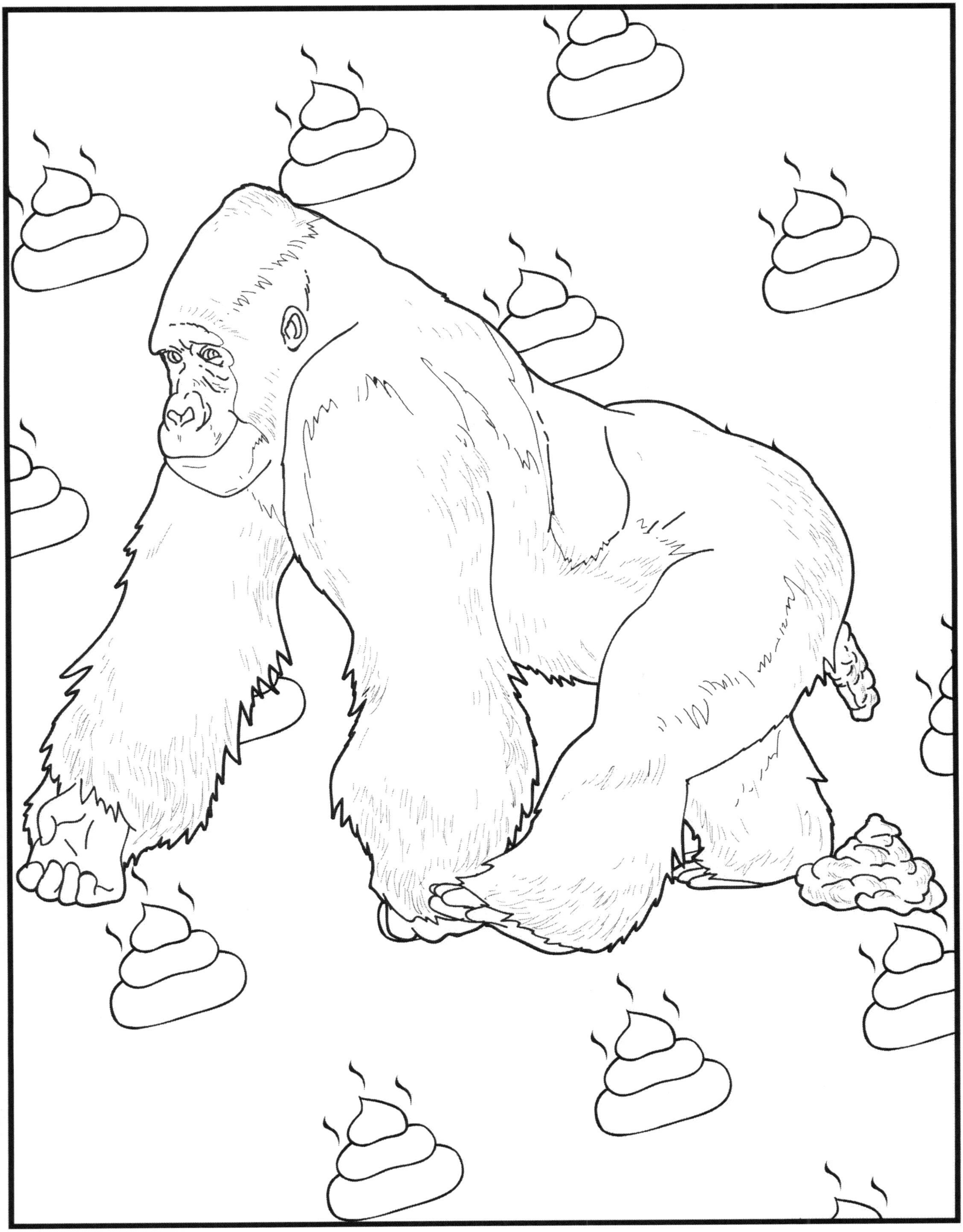

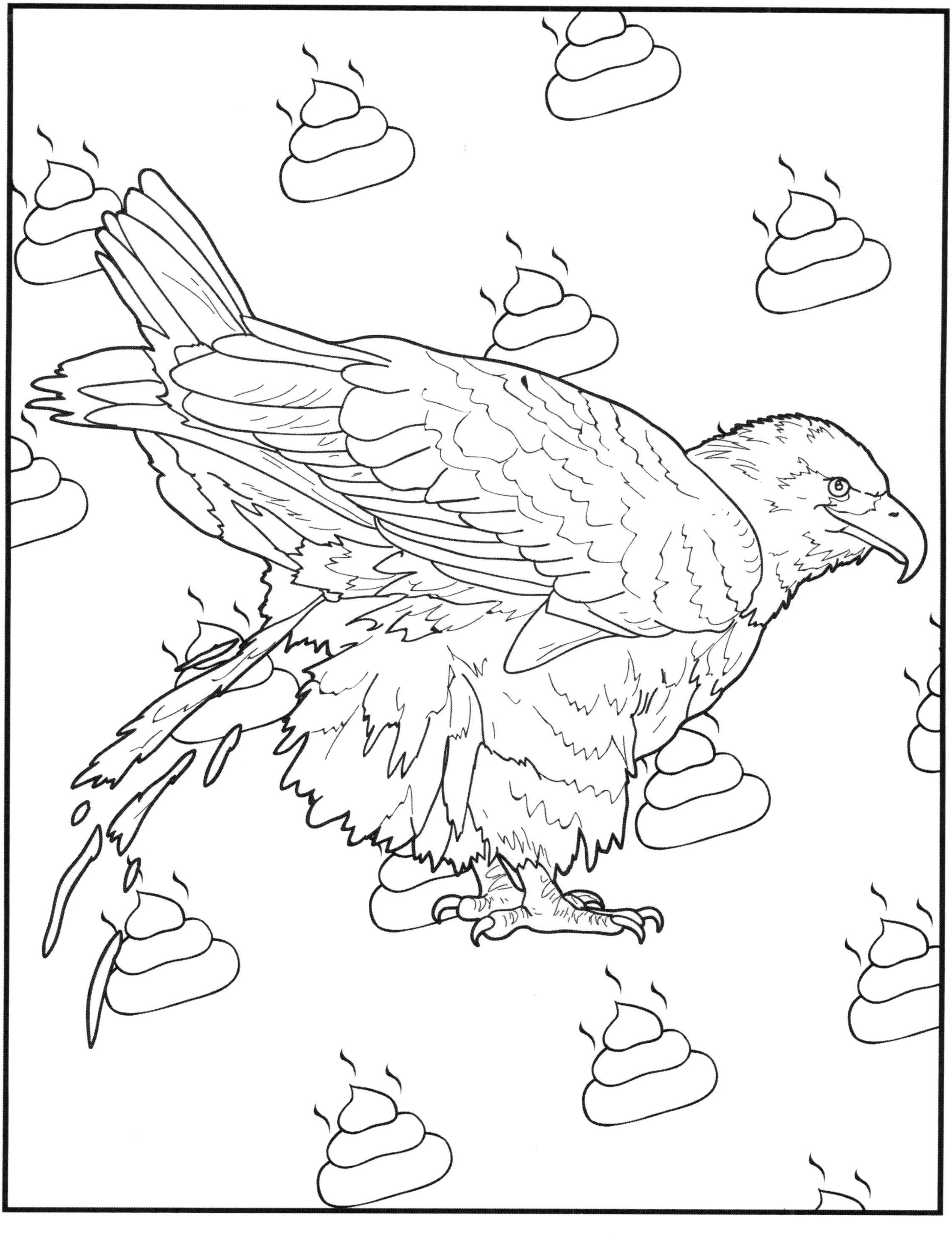

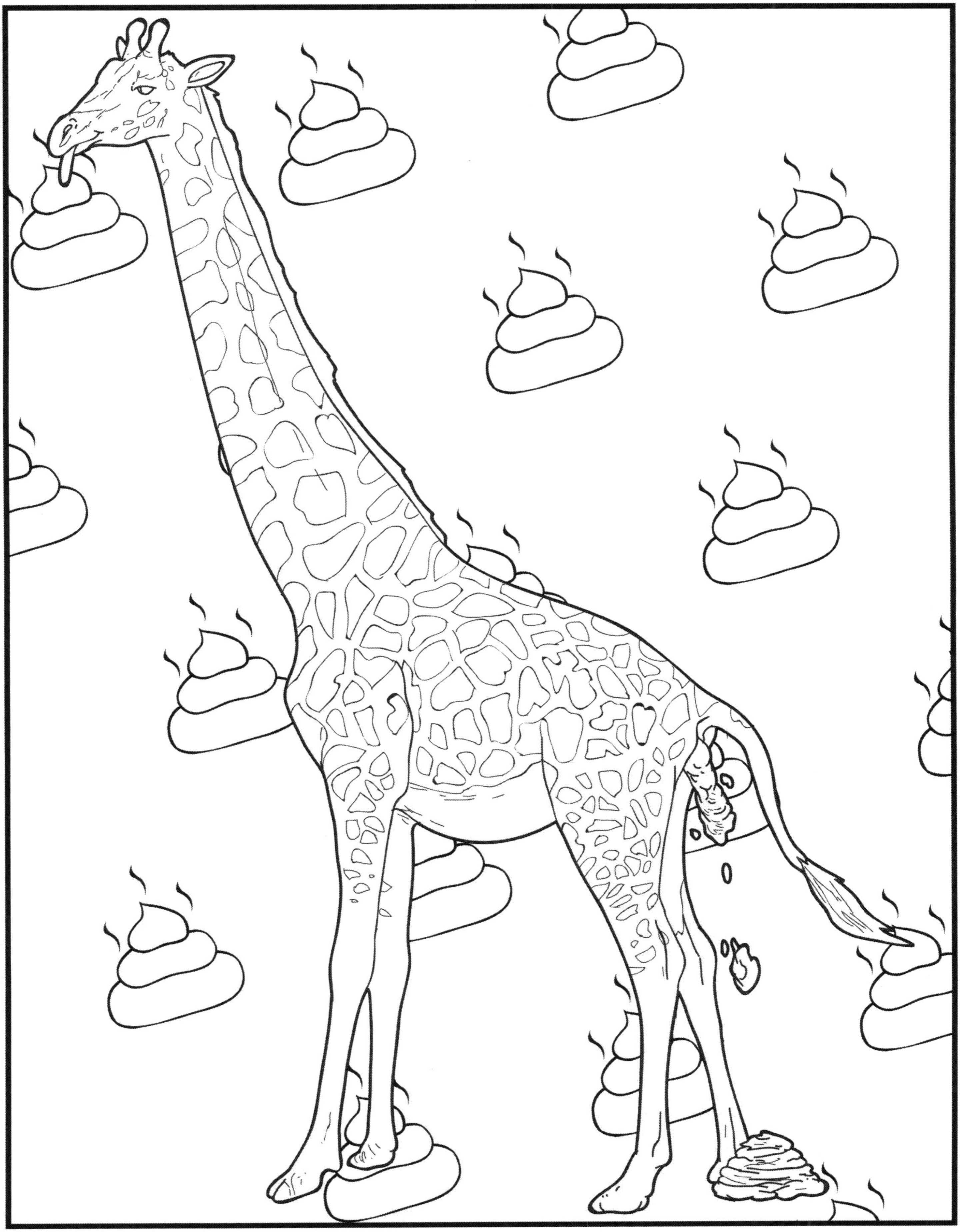

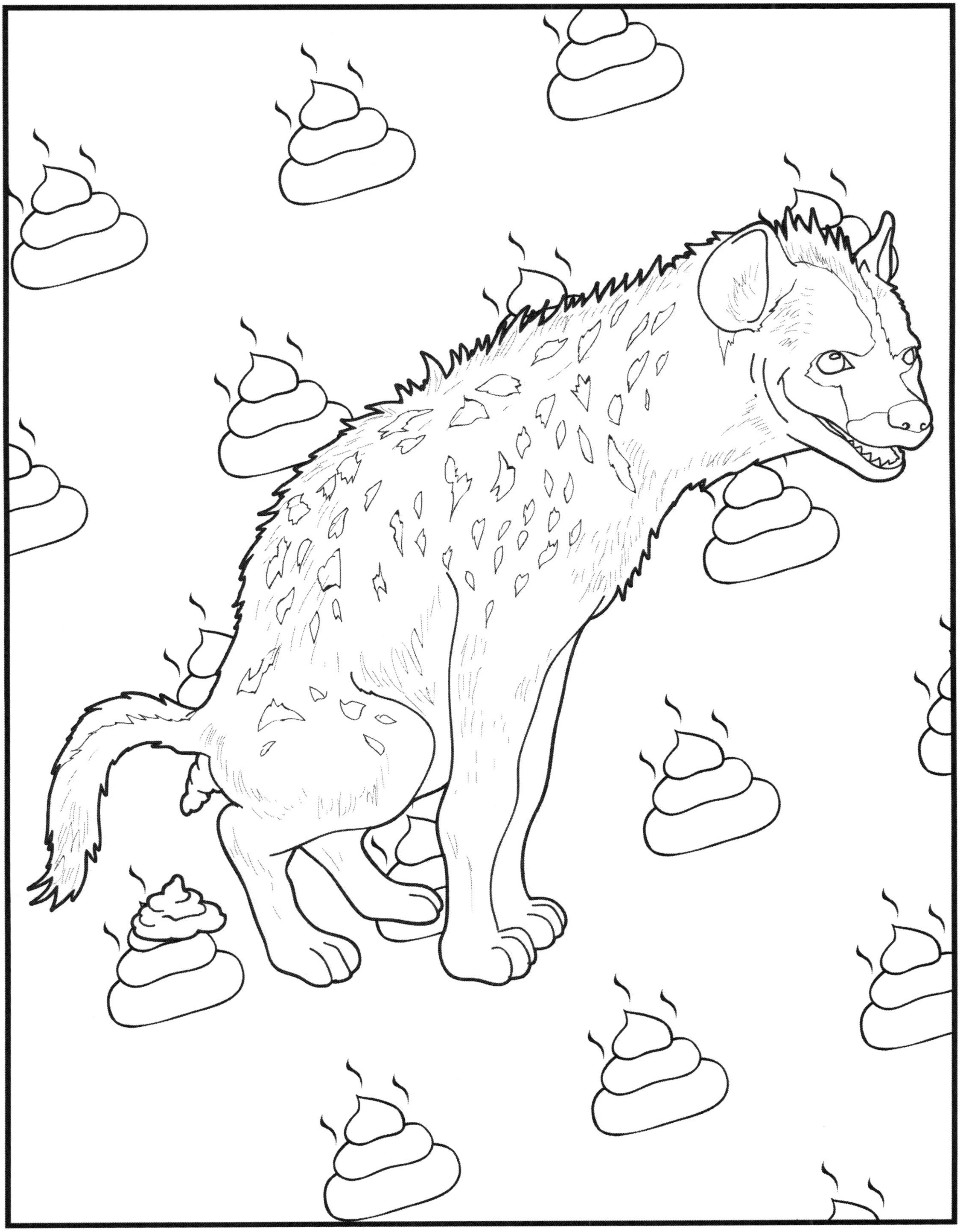

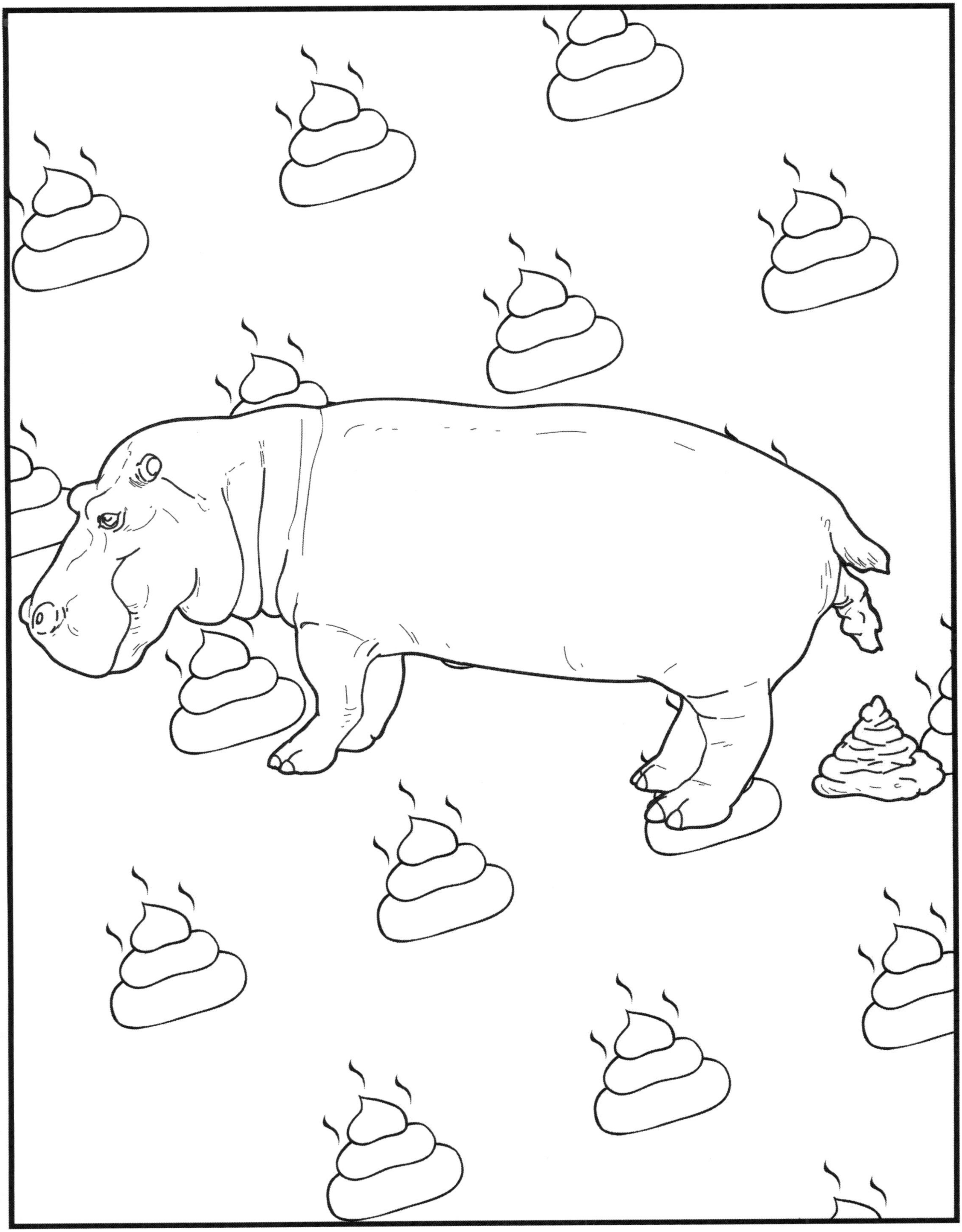

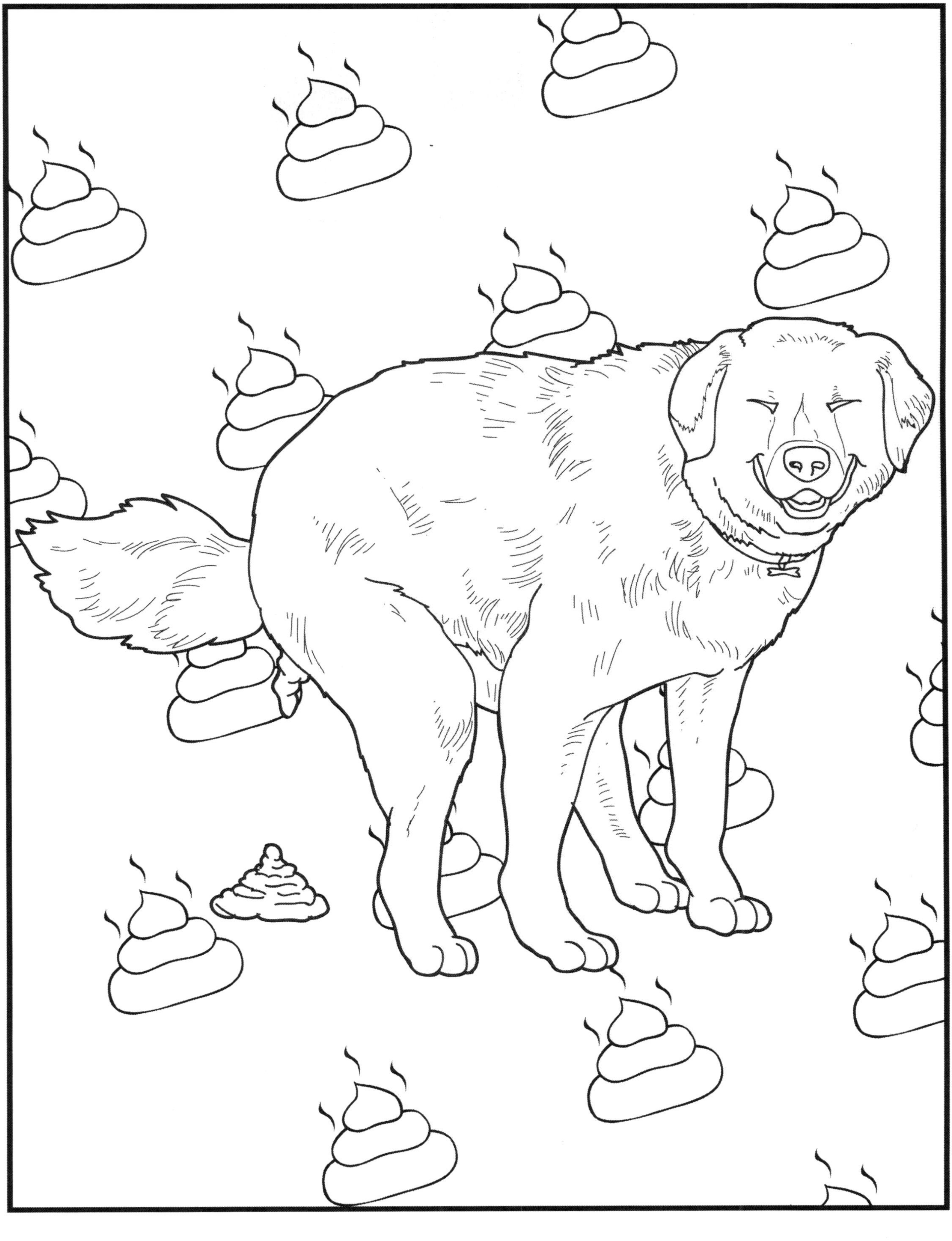

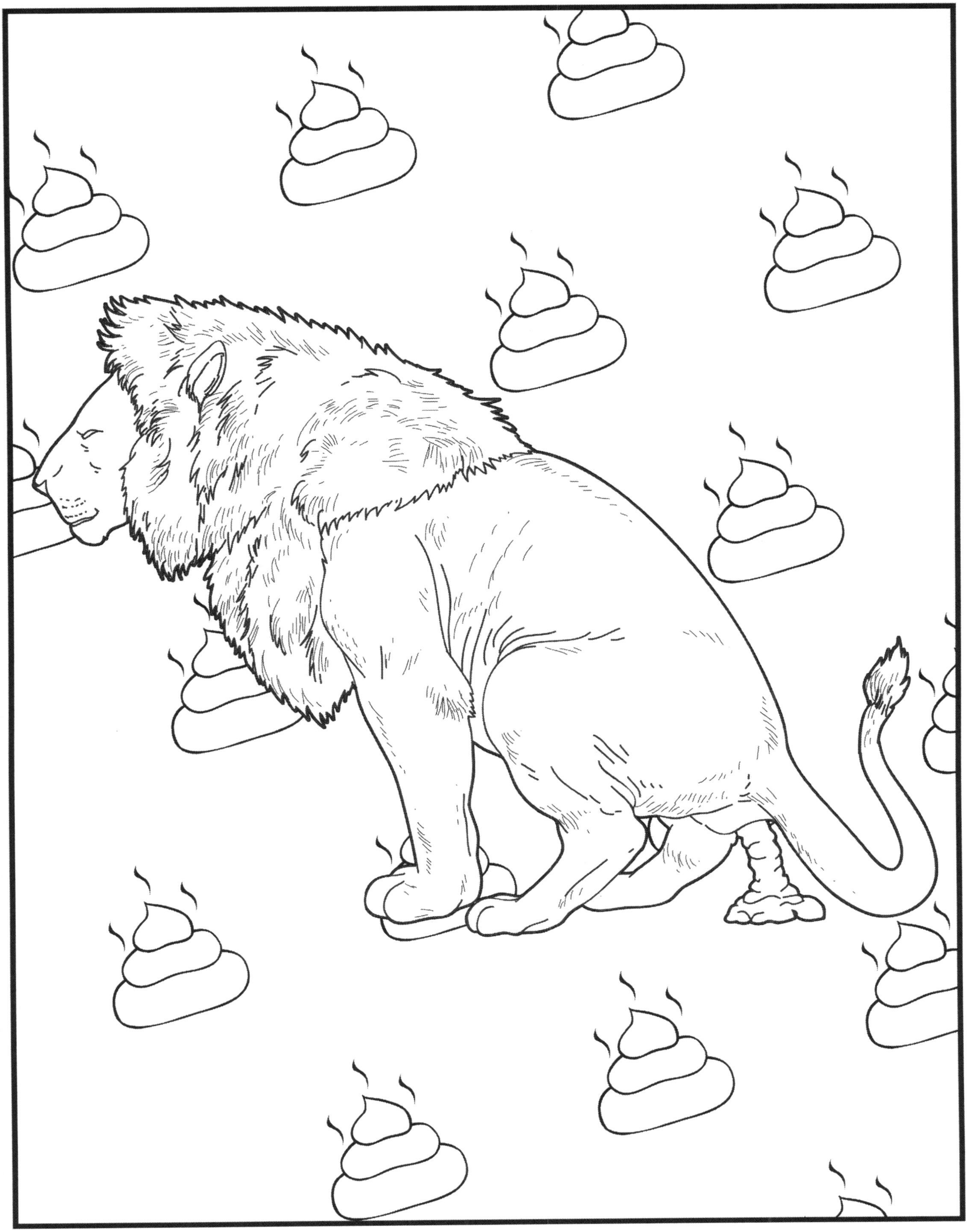

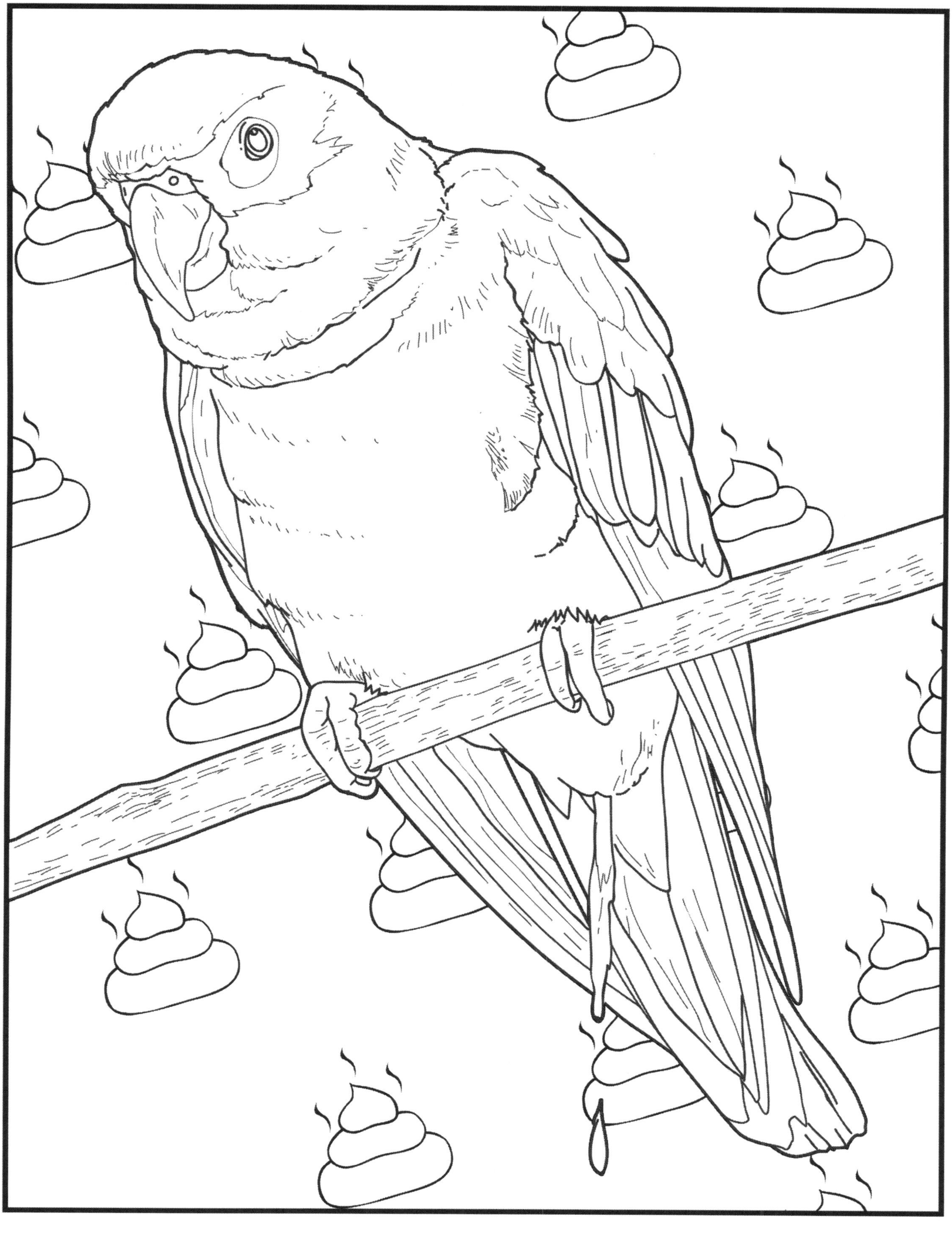

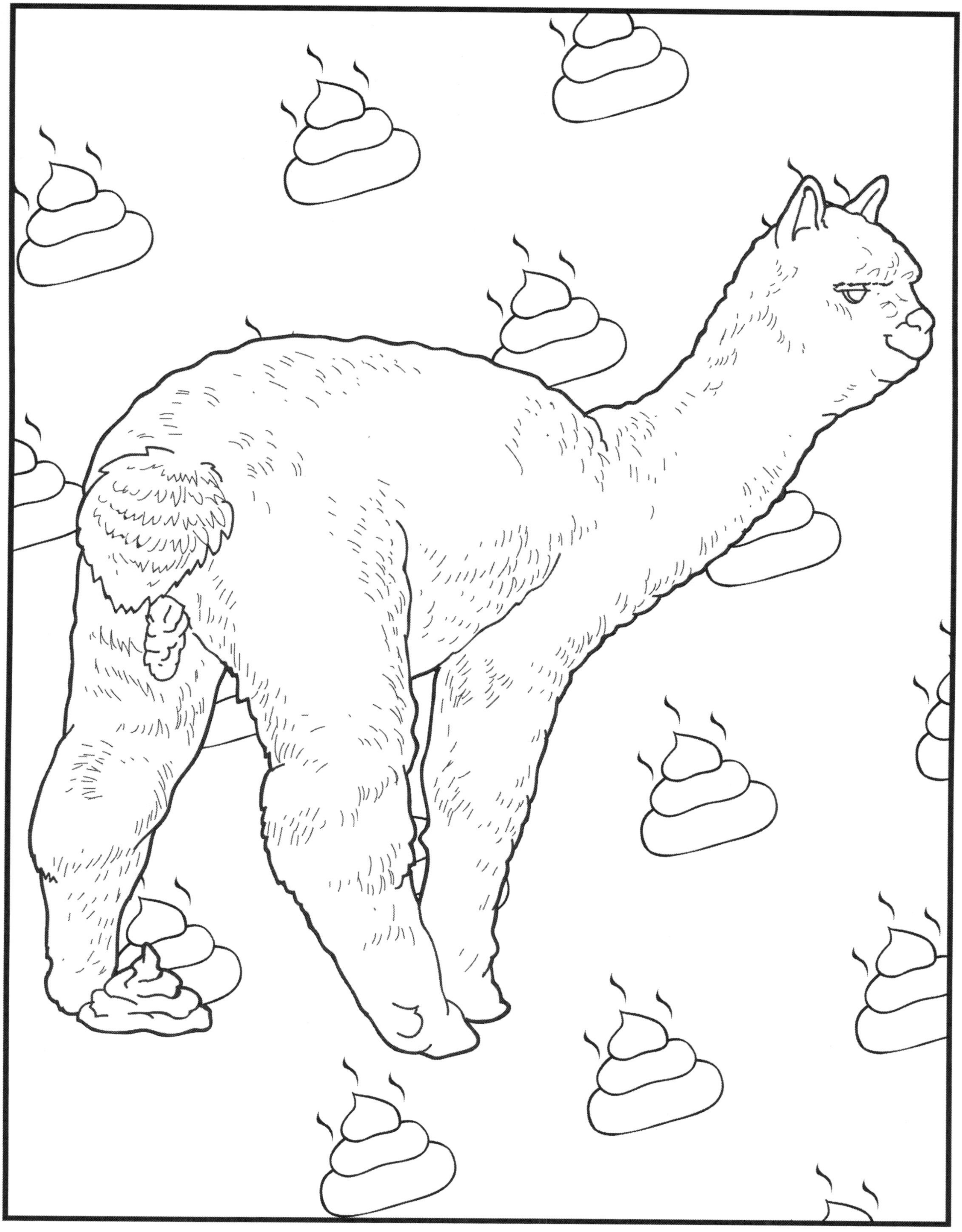

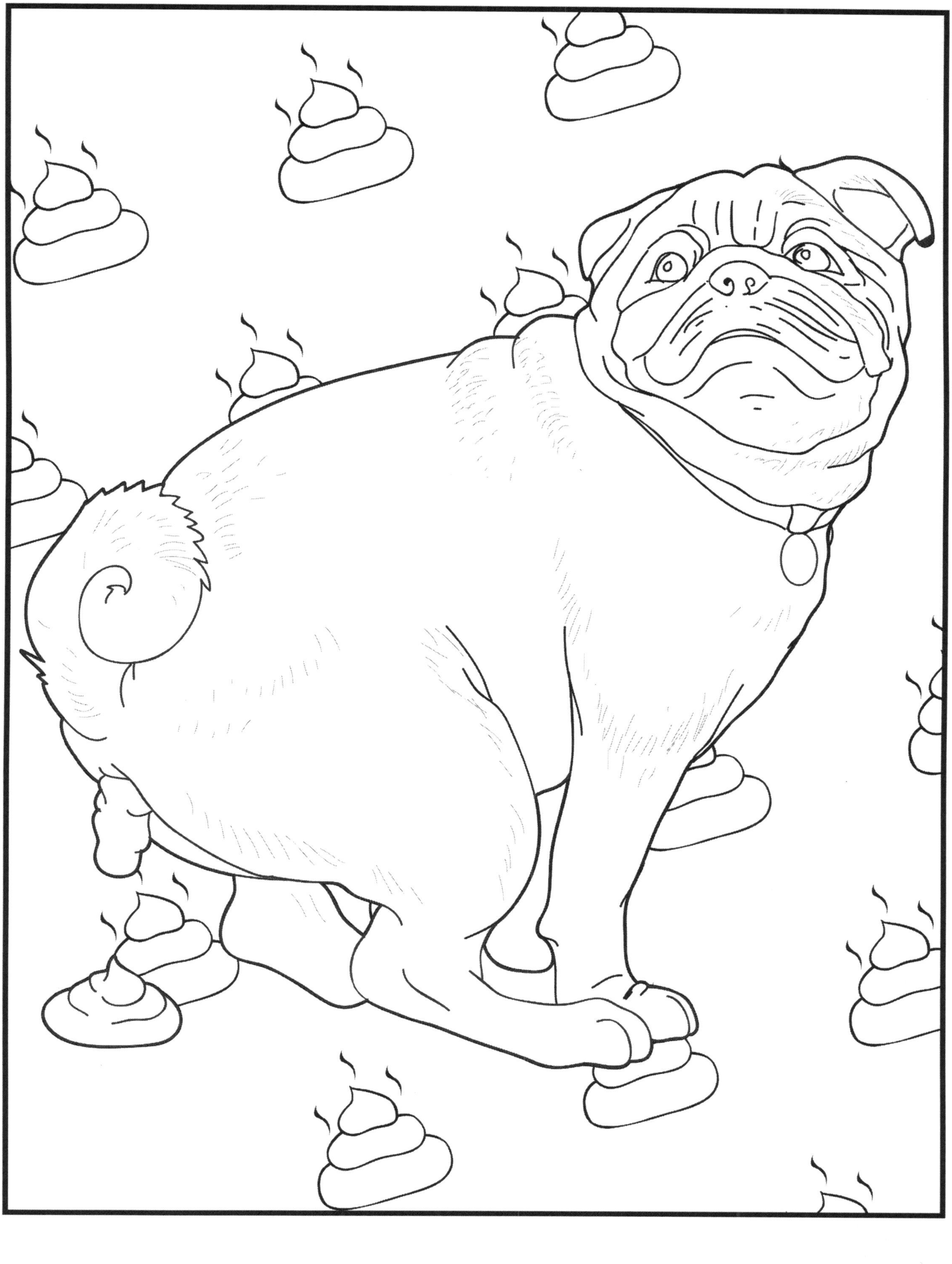

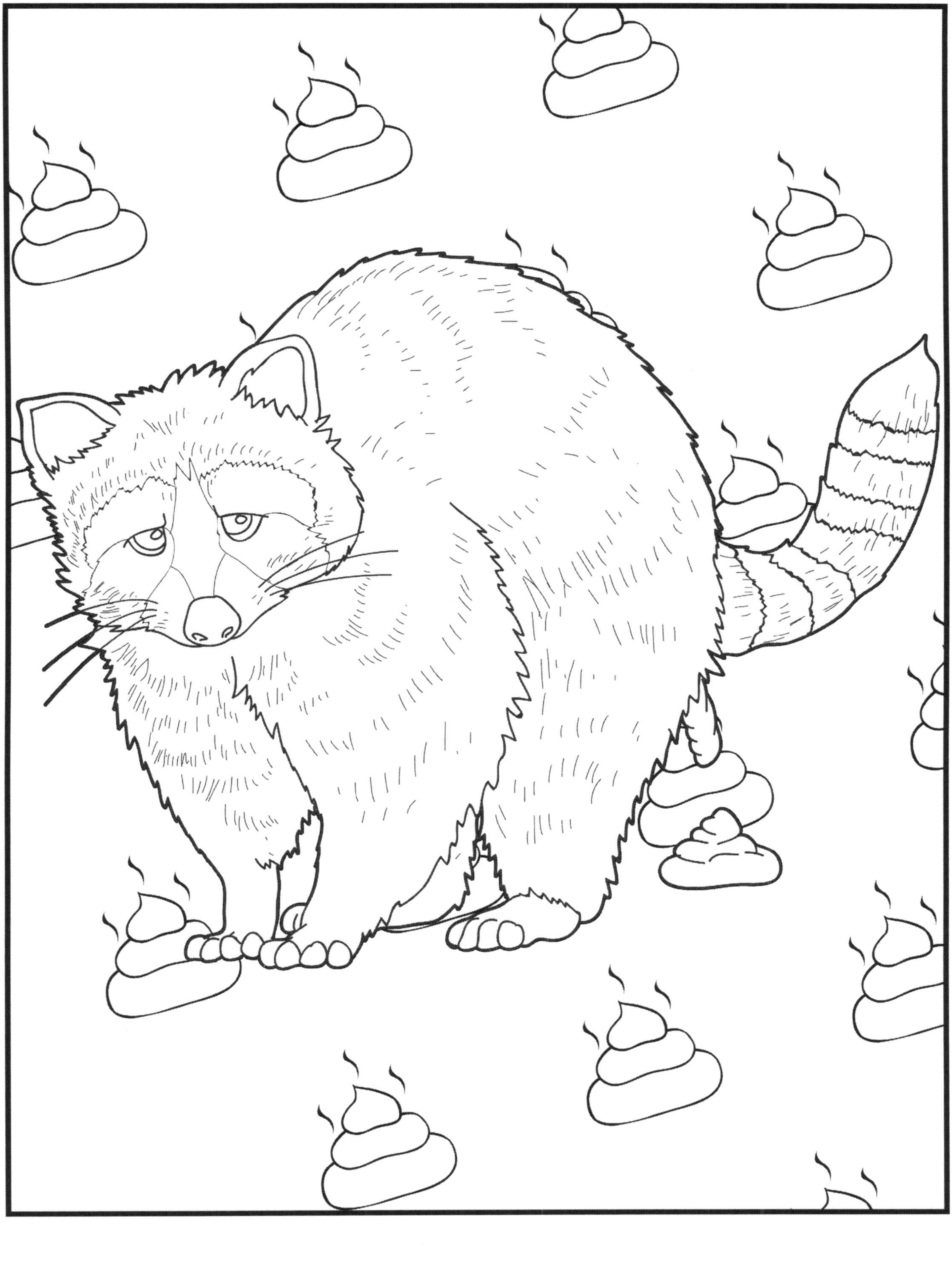

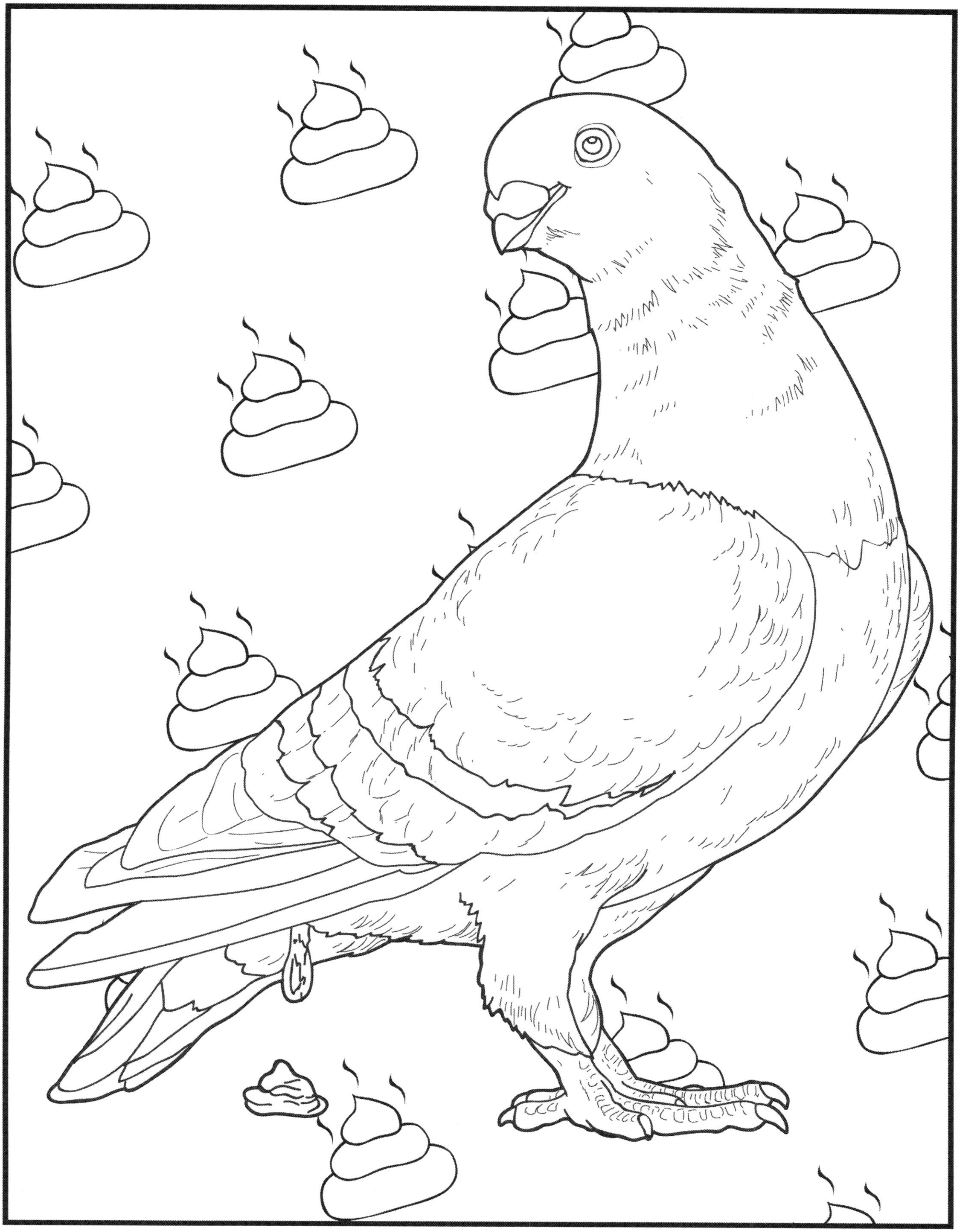

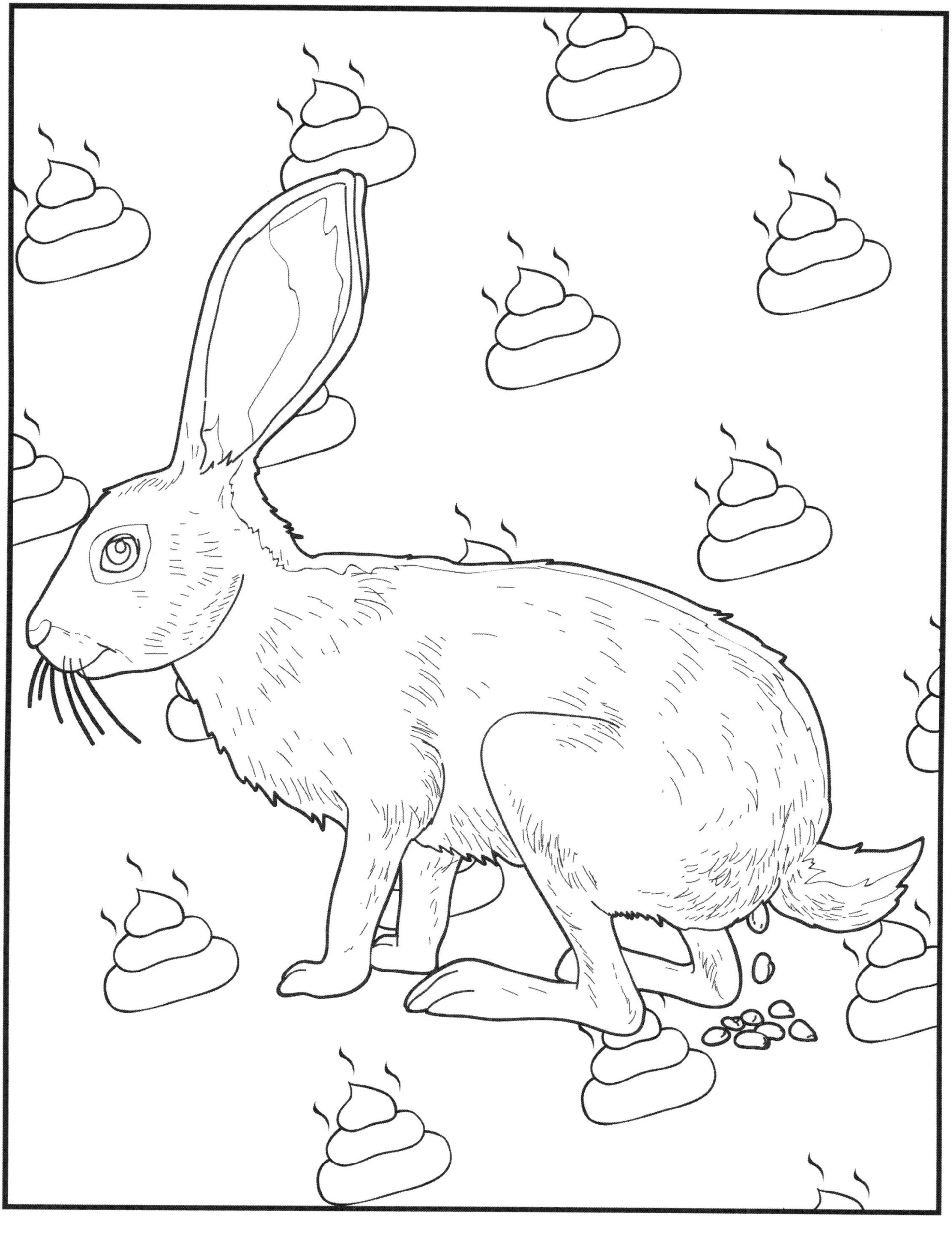

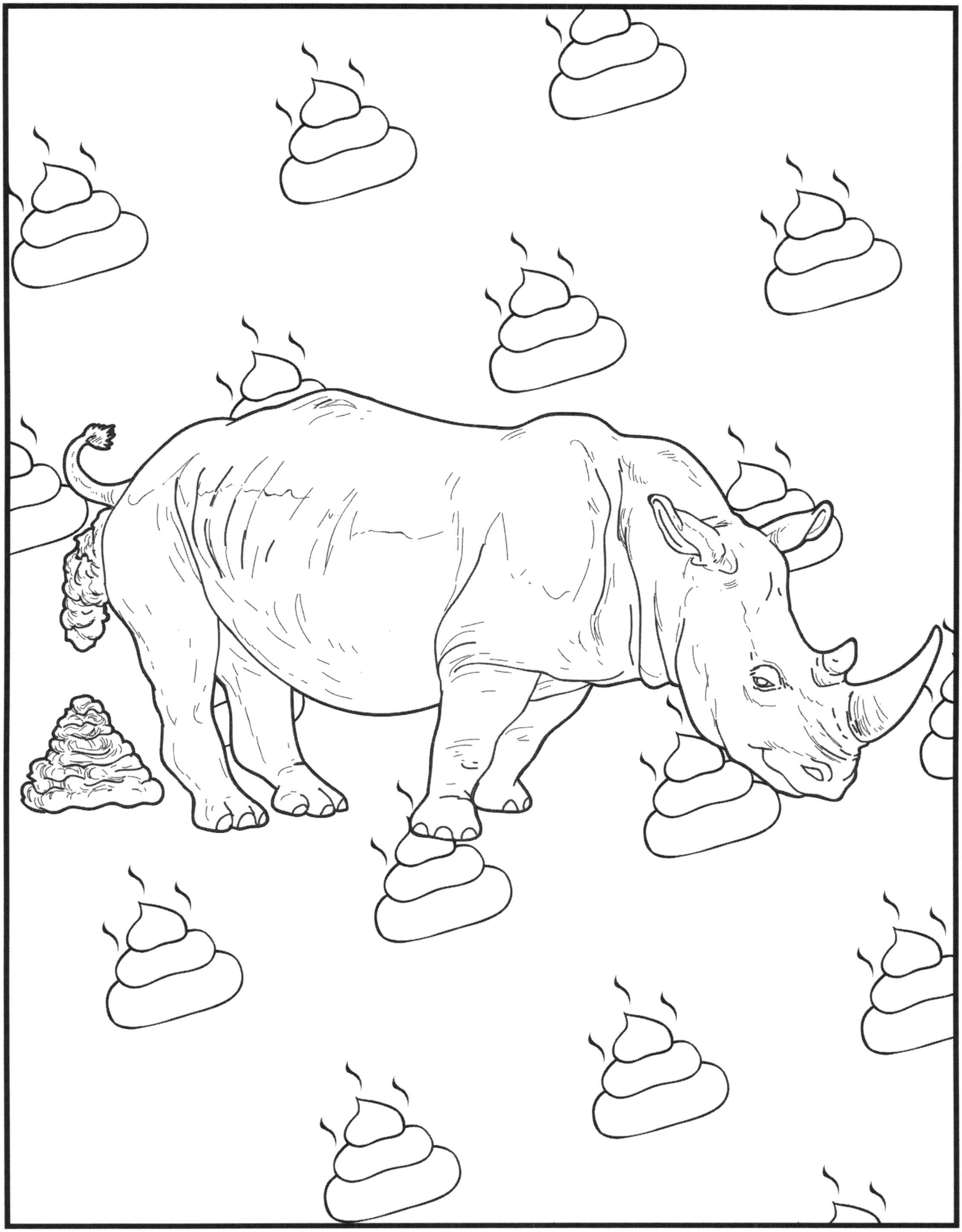

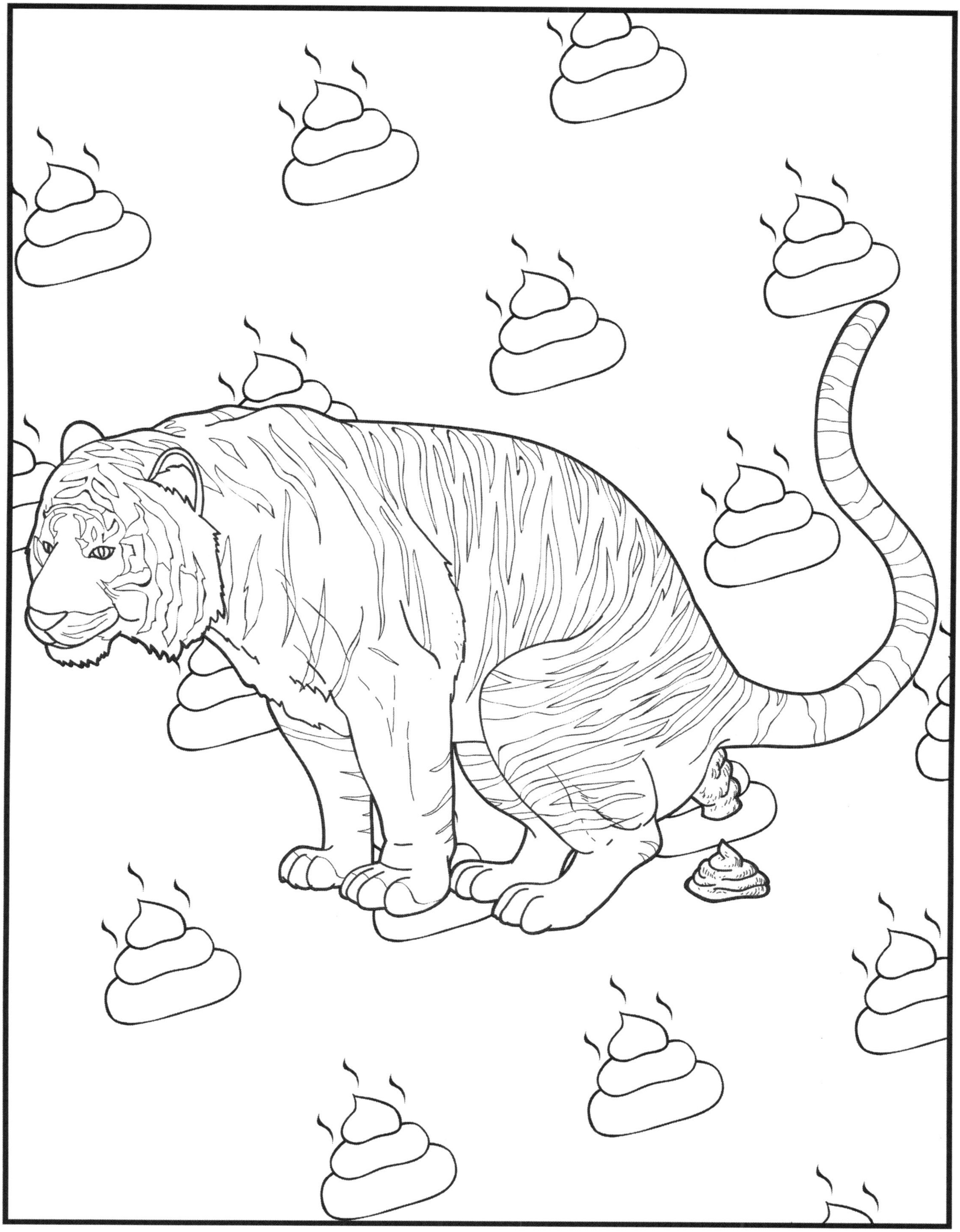

Made in the USA
San Bernardino, CA
10 December 2019

61241576R00024